TOO Mad to Trust™

Authors Josh Nathan and Linda Nathan   **Illustrated by Robin Mosler**

Open to Trust
a Friend

"Dedicated to all those who face their fears with eyes wide open."

TOO Mad to Trust

Too Mad To Trust
© 2015 Josh Nathan and Linda Nathan
NannyNoz Books
All Rights Reserved

Library of Congress 001941011
ISBN 978-0-9963316-0-9

It's a hot summer day and the sun is out to play.

4

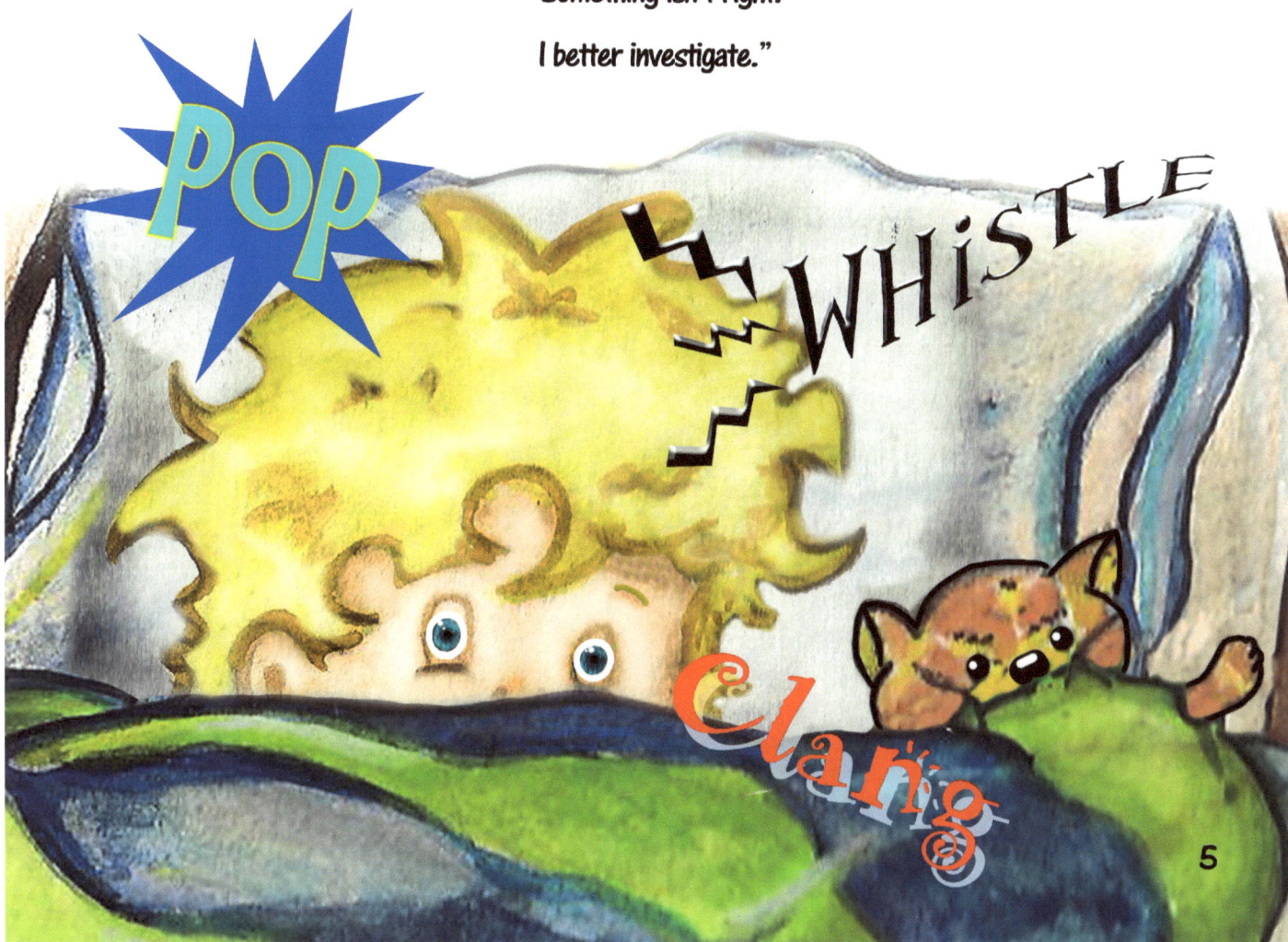

"What is THAT??"

"And where's Mom?

She usually wakes me up."

But not today.

"Something isn't right.

I better investigate."

POP

WHISTLE

Clang

5

"Why did Mom and Dad eat without me?
Did they forget about me? I have to go to school.
I'm going to be late."
But not today.

6

"Good morning, sleepyhead," Mom says to Andy when he enters the kitchen. "Dad already left and I have to go soon too."

"Why didn't you wake me up and won't I be late for school?" Andy asks.

"You don't have school today. It's the first day of your summer break," Mom reminds Andy.

"Actually, I was just testing you! You know that 'Detective Andy' is always on TOP of things."

"Well then, TOP Detective Andy better put something in the BOTTOM of his stomach," Mom says, grabbing waffles that suddenly pop out of the toaster. "After you're done eating, why don't you walk to Matt's house to see if he wants to play?"

Matt lives just a house away since moving to town a few months ago. The two make quite the pair! They joke together, ride the bus to school together, and eat lunch on the playground together. But Matt usually asks Andy to play. Andy doesn't like asking friends to play. He likes it better when they ask him. Wouldn't you, too?

"I have to go to work today so you guys can't play here," Andy's Mom tells him. "But Matt's Mom is home today. You can play there."

"What if Matt is busy?" Andy asks. "I know!!! What if you ask for me, Mom???"
"No, sweetie. I can't," his Mom says as she chuckles. "You're getting older. It's important for you to ask others to do things instead of waiting for them to ask you."

Andy is stumped. His Mom won't ask for him and he knows he can't stay home alone.

"What if Matt is already busy or doesn't want to play with me?" Andy wonders out loud. "Then what do I do, Mom? I'll be all alone. It will be your fault too because you didn't help me."

"I can live with that," his Mom replies as Andy sighs.

"Can't you come with me?" Andy pleads.

"Maybe another time," she says. "But not today."

Frustrated, Andy doesn't like the way this day is going already.

"Why is Mom making me ask Matt alone? Doesn't she realize that's scary?" Andy just doesn't understand.

He walks straight to Matt's door, but his mind turns toward his fears.

Andy navigates the short walk slowly, thinking…and thinking…and thinking about all the possibilities of what might happen when he gets to Matt's house.

Andy is thinking so much about what might happen that he doesn't realize he's reached Matt's door. Suddenly, it swings open and Matt appears.

"Hi, Andy," he says. "Want to play today?"

Andy is so upset at what Matt might say or do that he blurts out the first thing that comes to mind.

"Matt, I wouldn't play with you if you were the LAST person in the world!!!"

"What did I do???" Matt wonders with a look of surprise.

Andy's confused too for a minute until he feels an arm on his shoulder.

"It's Mom! She came after all! Oh no! I hope she didn't hear what I said," Andy thinks to himself, embarrassed. Though wishing was useless because everything Andy mumbled made its way in to his Mom's ears.

12

"Matt, your Mom and I thought the two of you might like to play together today. She's going to be home and I have to go to work. We thought the two of you would have fun here," she explains while Andy works to avoid Matt's gaze.

Andy's Mom leaves as abruptly as she came and Andy quickly forgets about his fears, playing in Matt's pool and games on Matt's new iPad. Andy doesn't have one and getting to play with it is a special treat.

let's go play

16

After what seems like barely any time at all, Andy's Mom is at the door again. Having so much fun, Andy can't believe the day is already over.

That night, Andy's parents ask him if he had a good time with Matt and he tells them all about their adventures. Then Dad asks Andy why he was afraid to ask Matt to play.

"Do you think Matt is your friend?" Dad asks.

"Yes," Andy replies.

"Do you trust Matt?" Dad asks.

"Yes," Andy answers again.

"Did the two of you have a fight?" Dad asks.

"No," says Andy, who is confused but not angry, frustrated without knowing why, and disappointed yet lost in thought again.

Andy can't figure out why he said such a terrible, horrible, awful thing!

19

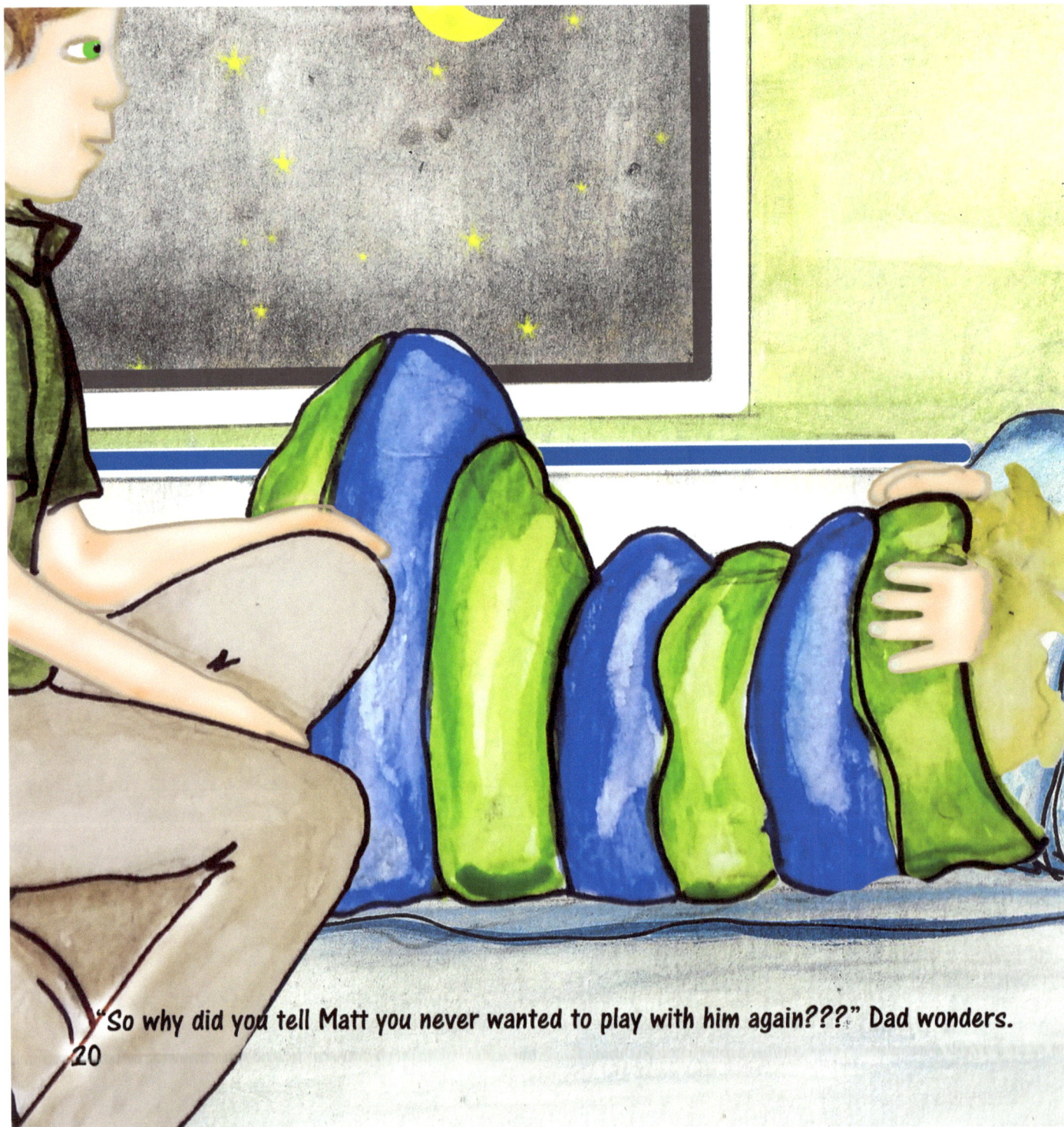

"So why did you tell Matt you never wanted to play with him again???" Dad wonders.

"It's really Mom's fault because she wouldn't ask Matt to play for me. So I started thinking of everything Matt might say or do and I guess I got worked up. What else can I say?" Andy asks his Dad.

"Andy, you let your mind play games on you. You let fear question your friendship with Matt. Fear is a powerful thing. It can rule, and RUIN, your life if you let it. Or you can choose to control your fears so only you decide how you want to act," Dad explains to Andy.

"I know you think Matt is your friend. I know you have fun together. I know you were just afraid," Dad continues. "But you have to face your fears. Everybody has to at some point and, at your age, it's time to start," Dad says. "It's like learning how to ride a bike."

"Do you and Matt have fun together?" Dad asks.

"Yah," Andy says.

"Do you think if you need help, Matt would help you?" Dad asks.

"Yah," Andy says.

"Maybe you need to think about what it means to be a friend because REAL friends trust each other. It doesn't sound like you really trust Matt yet..."

"Friends can be mean. So how do I know when to trust someone, Dad?" Andy asks.

"Let me put it to you this way," Dad says. "If Matt is sad, would you try to cheer him up?"
"Yah."

"Would you bring him to our house if no one was at his?"
"Yah."

"Would you share some of your toys like Matt shared his iPad?"
"Yah."

"Andy, those are all things friends do for each other when they trust each other. Friends can be mean sometimes without meaning it, just like you didn't mean the mean things you said to Matt today. Friends trust and help each other—that's what it means to be a friend." Dad adds. "Think about it, Andy. Goodnight and I love you," Dad says as he closes the bedroom door, leaving it just a little open.

Andy's thoughts swim with ideas of friendship, trust, doubt, and possibilities.

As he drifts off to sleep, Andy decides to face his fears and trust his friends. They may not always help him the same way his parents do. But, if they're really his friends, they'll try to protect him too! Matt is a good friend because he didn't get mad at Andy when Andy accidentally got mad at him.

Before Andy knows it, he enters a world less afraid than when he woke up this morning.

The mind's a funny thing. A cat can become a lion; a backyard, a jungle; and a detective who may lose his way eventually gets to the bottom of things!

It's summer and Andy knows it's going to be

GREAT

because the sky's the limit!

Thinking About What You Have Read

1. What do trust and fear mean to you?

2. Why is Andy afraid to trust his friend?

3. What are a few of the things Andy and Matt do together?

4. Can you identify each of the seven creatures in Andy's dream after he falls asleep?

5. What does Andy learn from his Dad near the end of the story?

Making Connections

How do you determine who you should, or shouldn't, trust?

www.ingramcontent.com/pod-product-compliance
Lightning Source LLC
Chambersburg PA
CBHW041222040426
42443CB00002B/59